A Note to Parents and Teachers

The *Dorling Kindersley* Readers is a compelling reading programme for children, developed with a leading literacy expert.

The series combines lively pictures with engaging, easy-to-read stories guaranteed to capture a child's interest, while developing his or her reading skills, general knowledge and love of reading.

The four levels of Readers are aimed at different reading abilities, enabling you to choose the books that are exactly right for each child.

Level 1 – Beginning to Read
Level 2 – Beginning to Read Alone
Level 3 – Reading Alone
Level 4 – Proficient Readers

The "normal" age at which a child begins to read can be anywhere from three to eight years old, so these levels are intended only as a general guideline.

No matter which level you select, you can be sure that you are helping your child learn to read, then read to learn!

Dorling DK Kindersley

LONDON, NEW YORK, SYDNEY, DELHI, PARIS, MUNICH and JOHANNESBURG

Senior Editor Cynthia O'Neill
Editor Rebecca Knowles
Senior Managing Art Editor Cathy Tincknell
Publishing Manager Karen Dolan
Senior DTP Designer Andrew O'Brien
Production Nicola Torode

First published in Great Britain in 2000 by
Dorling Kindersley Limited,
9 Henrietta Street,
Covent Garden, London WC2E 8PS

2 4 6 8 10 9 7 5 3 1

© 2000 World Championship Wrestling.
A Time Warner Company. All Rights Reserved.

www.wcw.com

All rights reserved. No part of this publication may be reproduced, stored in a retrieval system, or transmitted in any form or by any means, electronic, mechanical, photocopying, recording, or otherwise, without the prior written permission of the copyright owner.

A CIP catalogue record for this book is available from the British Library.

ISBN 0-7513-2792-1

Colour reproduction by Dot Gradations, UK
Printed and bound in China

Illustrations by Paul Trevillion.
The publisher would like to thank the following for their kind permission to reproduce their images:
Ronald Grant Archive: 44b.
Special photographers
Dave King, Andy Crawford and Richard Leeney

All other photographic images provided by World Championship Wrestling, Inc.
Special thanks to Joseph Lester, WCW, Inc.

see our complete
catalogue at
www.dk.com

Contents

Rising star	5
Explosive entrance	8
Signature moves	10
WCW debut	12
First championship	14
World champion	18
Who's next?	22
The streak ends	28
The Rematch	30
Greatest foes	32
Toughest fights	38
Fitness routine	40
On screen	44
Big man, big heart	46
Glossary	48

DK DORLING KINDERSLEY *READERS* WCW

GOING FOR GOLDBERG

Written by Michael Teitelbaum

PROFICIENT **4** READERS

DK
A Dorling Kindersley Book

Rising star

"Goldberg! Goldberg! Goldberg!"

The crowd chants his name. The mountain of muscle they call Goldberg is wrestling's greatest star. But where did his story begin? And how did he come to take World Championship Wrestling by storm?

William Scott Goldberg grew up in Tulsa, Oklahoma. He showed great athletic talent as a boy and in high school he was a star American football player. College scouts from all around the country came to watch him play.

Goldberg accepted a college scholarship to the University of Georgia. He played for their football team, the Georgia Bulldogs, and became captain of the defensive team. He played so well that he won individual awards.

He also studied hard and earned a degree in psychology.

Fearless
As teenagers, Goldberg and his two brothers loved to fly gliders and acrobatic planes. This, along with his football training, helped build his "no fear" attitude.

Football player
During college, Goldberg was a member of the "Junkyard Dog Club". Only the football team's best defensive players could join this select group!

Teams
As a professional footballer, Goldberg was first signed up by the Los Angeles Rams, and then went on to play for the Atlanta Falcons.

Panthers
After his career with the Falcons ended, Goldberg joined the newly formed Carolina Panthers in 1995. However, injuries kept him from ever playing with the team.

After college, Goldberg became a professional football player. He played in the US National Football League, or NFL, until 1994, when injuries forced him to retire.

What would this powerful athlete do next?

Goldberg was a formidable sight on the football field

Goldberg was introduced to the world of professional wrestling through a series of chance meetings. His brother Mike shared a house with the wrestler Ric Flair. Then, while working out in the gym, Goldberg became friends with the wrestlers Sting and Lex Luger. They encouraged him to try his hand at wrestling. Finally, while out to dinner one night in Atlanta, Goldberg met Diamond Dallas Page (DDP).

"I took one look at Goldberg and told him, 'you need to be with us in WCW'," Page says.

Fortunately for wrestling fans, Goldberg followed DDP's advice.

Before *we* follow Goldberg's rise to the top of WCW, let's look at the special style and unique moves that have made him such a great champion.

DDP
The popular wrestler Diamond Dallas Page actually started in wrestling as a manager, developing the talents of others. He made his own debut as a wrestler in 1991 and has since become one of the great stars of WCW.

Explosive entrance

His theme music blasts from the speakers in the arena. The crowd rises to its feet and cheers. They know Goldberg is about to make his entrance. And what an entrance it is!

Jimmy Hart
Goldberg's theme was produced by Jimmy Hart. As well as being a famous wrestling manager, Hart is a rock musician. He used to play in a rock band called the Gentrys.

It begins when Doug Dellinger, WCW's head of security, knocks on the locker room door. Beside him stand two security guards.

The door bursts open and Goldberg marches towards the ring. The security guards walk on either side of him – to protect everyone else from the most dangerous man in championship wrestling!

As Goldberg enters the arena, fireworks explode from the floor. He is bathed in sparks and smoke. As the fireworks end, Goldberg blows out a stream of smoke.

He charges into the ring, throwing punches in the air, while the sound of explosions fills the arena. The crowd knows he's ready for action as he bellows his catchphrase: "Who's next?!"

Special events
WCW stages 12 pay-per-view spectaculars each year, such as Souled Out, which takes place every February.

Muscle mountain
Goldberg is 1.9 m tall and weighs 129 kg.

Signature moves

Goldberg's style inside the ring can be defined by one word – aggressive! He's even been known to take on two opponents at a time.

But he is most famous for his finishing moves: the Spear and the Jackhammer. When the champ unleashes these moves, no one is left standing...except the crowd, up on its feet and cheering!

Family ties
How does Goldberg's family feel when they see him in action, ready to flatten an opponent? He says that at first they were dismayed by his decision to be a wrestler, but now they are his biggest fans.

Goldberg flattens Sting with the Spear

The Spear is taken from the days when Goldberg played American football. He launches himself into a football tackle, aimed right at his opponent's mid-section. The other wrestler hits the mat with a crunch.

Now Goldberg is ready to perform the Jackhammer. This is a devastating finishing move and usually it ends the match.

First, Goldberg lifts his opponent into the air and carries him around the ring. Then he leaps up and slams his victim to the mat.

Finally, Goldberg turns his body, and lands on his opponent with nearly 130 kilos of muscle.

Match over!

Goldberg wins!

Goldberg slams Ernest Miller with a Jackhammer.

The ring
The average WCW wrestling "ring" is in fact a square, which measures about six metres across!

Power Plant
Each month, about 15 people take part in a three-day trial to become WCW wrestlers. Up to three people are accepted for the six-month training programme at the Power Plant.

WCW debut

The Goldberg phenomenon began on September 22, 1997. That was when Goldberg made his first TV appearance, on Monday Nitro, WCW's Monday-night wrestling programme.

Goldberg had spent the previous months at the Power Plant, the training centre where would-be wrestlers prepare to enter the action-packed world of WCW. Now, after intensive training, Goldberg was ready to make his debut.

His opponent was the veteran wrestler Hugh Morrus. For all his experience, Morrus was completely unprepared for the powerhouse he was about to face.

Goldberg climbed into the ring. He stared coldly at Morrus as the bell rang to begin the match.

As Goldberg begins a fight, every bit of his concentration is focused on the job at hand.

Morrus wonders what went wrong, as Goldberg is declared the winner.

It only took a couple of minutes for Goldberg to get the upper hand. Moments later, the match was over. Goldberg had demolished Morrus.

Victory number one was already under his belt.

Hugh Morrus
They say Morrus is an animal in the ring! He's known for his hyena-like laugh and his battle technique, which has been compared to a charging rhino.

nWo
The nWo (New World Order) was a renegade group of wrestlers who continually tried to take over WCW. They were formed by Scott Hall and Kevin Nash, and their members included Hulk Hogan and Scott Steiner. They often used tricks to win a match – such as taking weapons into the ring.

Spring Stampede
When a wrestler competes on a pay-per-view event like Spring Stampede, he knows he's made the big time.

First championship

After this first triumph, Goldberg continued to win match after match. He beat his opponents with ease, because his determination, strength and devastating finishing moves were too much for them.

Soon, Goldberg was meeting mid-ranked wrestlers. He powered his way through them, as well.

It was around this time that Goldberg had a run-in with the rebel wrestlers known as the nWo. The nWo had realized that Goldberg was on his way to the top – and so the bad boys of wrestling thought it was time to intimidate him. Before he had ever battled an nWo member – in a WCW match, Goldberg was attacked outside the ring by a swarm of nWo thugs.

This didn't stop him. Goldberg continued to wow the WCW fans.

During one amazing spell, from 26 March to 30 March, 1998, he fought veteran wrestler Jerry Flynn every night, in five different arenas. Goldberg demolished Flynn every time!

Bash at the Beach
This pay-per-view event takes place every July.

Goldberg and Flynn battle it out.

15

Belt of pride
When a wrestler wins a championship, the WCW presents him with a belt. The belt is rumoured to be made of solid gold, with leather straps, and is said to weigh about five kilos.

The Flock
The members of Raven's Flock were Saturn, Reese, Lodi, Sick Boy, Horace, Riggs, Van Hammer and Kidman (*above*).

During Spring Stampede 1998, Goldberg had a major victory over a wrestler called Saturn. Saturn took the defeat badly. This was the start of a long-running feud between the two men.

On April 20, 1998, Goldberg took on the wrestler named Raven, for the WCW US Championship. At the time, Raven was leader of a group of wrestlers called the Flock.

It was an exciting, close-fought match. The advantage seesawed back and forth and it was impossible to say who would win.

At one point, when things were going well for Goldberg, other members of the Flock jumped into the ring to help Raven. Goldberg defeated each one.

Finally, Goldberg finished Raven off with the Jackhammer.

The fight was over. Goldberg was the new US champion.

17

Many Champions
There are five different categories of championship in WCW: World, US, Tag team, Hardcore and Cruiserweight.

La Parka
During May and June 1998, Goldberg won 16 matches, including a victory over La Parka, a Mexican wrestler whose name means "the Mask".

World champion

Goldberg's feud with Saturn continued after the new champion had won his first belt. In May and June 1998, Goldberg fought and defeated Saturn ten times!

Goldberg also proved himself to be a loyal friend at this time. During one Monday Nitro, his friend Kevin Greene was attacked by fellow wrestlers the Giant and Curt Hennig.

At the time, Greene wasn't even in the ring; he was giving an interview!

Later that night, while Greene wrestled the Giant, Hennig jumped into the ring. He unfairly helped the Giant attack Greene.

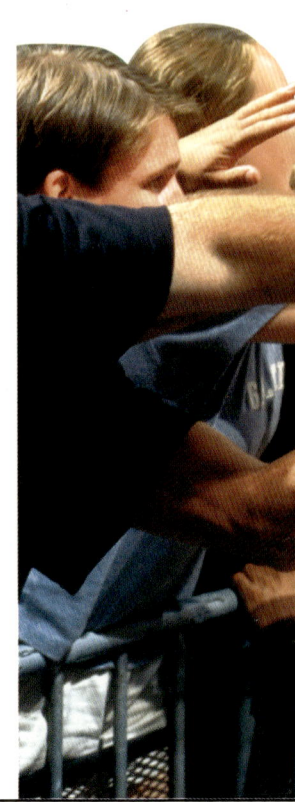

Goldberg rushed to the rescue. He jumped into the ring, quickly disposing of the Giant and Hennig.

Throughout the spring and early summer of 1998, Goldberg tore through WCW like a tornado. Finally, it was announced that the young challenger would face Hulk Hogan (then known as Hollywood Hogan) for the WCW World Championship.

With every victory, Goldberg made more and more fans.

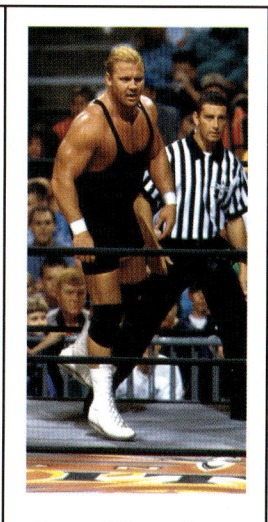

Curt Hennig Hennig made his debut in 1979. He has been a major wrestling star ever since.

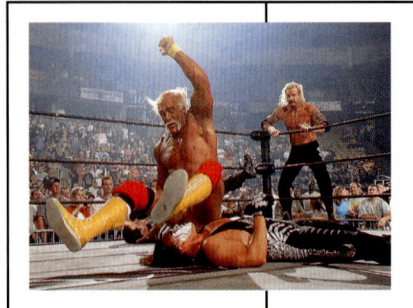

Hogan's Legdrop
Hulk Hogan's legdrop begins when his opponent is already lying on the mat. First Hulk runs off the ropes. Then he jumps up and drops a leg over his rival's face and neck, pinning him to the mat.

Victory roar
When Goldberg wins a match, he often turns to the crowd and gives a mighty roar of triumph.

On July 6, 1998, Goldberg was ready to take on Hogan. But first, he had a nasty surprise. Before he could wrestle the champ, Goldberg was made to fight Scott Hall, one of Hogan's nWo allies. It was a tough match, but Goldberg won.

Finally, Goldberg met Hogan. At first, Hogan dominated the fight. He hit Goldberg with two legdrops, but he couldn't pin the challenger.

Goldberg kicked out of the legdrops. He nailed Hogan with a Spear, and followed with the Jackhammer for "the pin".

Hogan was beaten. The WCW had a new World Champion!

Monday Nitro Many of Goldberg's matches have appeared on Monday Nitro, the WCW programme which first appeared on US television in 1995.

Who's next?

Goldberg started winning WCW matches in 1997. Little did anyone know then that this would be the start of the longest winning streak in wrestling history. Eventually, Goldberg won 175 fights in a row.

As WCW World Champion, Goldberg had to take on all challengers, and watch out for the nWo, too. Hogan's nWo friends were looking for revenge after Hogan's defeat.

Once, while Goldberg was busy in the arena trashing Brian Adams, the nWo were busy trashing Goldberg's dressing room! The champ didn't let such tactics affect his focus.

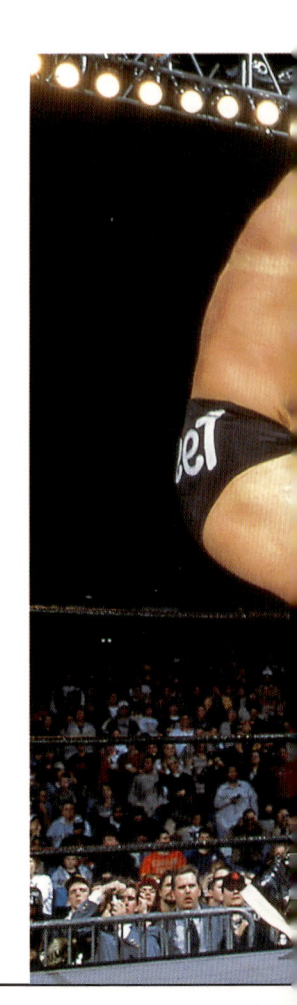

Music fan
You might be surprised to learn that Goldberg is a country rock music fan. One of his favourite groups is the Charlie Daniels Band.

Fall Brawl
At Fall Brawl 98 DDP tried to flee his clash with Goldberg. The champ stopped him!

He concentrated on beating everyone in sight.

Next, the nWo ganged up on Goldberg's friend DDP during a match. Goldberg tried to come to the rescue, but the Giant prevented him.

Goldberg now had it in for the Giant. He wanted to beat him.

Brian Adams
Adams joined WCW in 1998, teaming up with the nWo right away. His tag team partners have included Curt Hennig and Sting.

Scott Hall
A co-founder of the nWo, Hall has been a constant thorn in Goldberg's side. Their clashes have been among the most exciting, and controversial, in WCW.

At the Battle Royale in the summer of 1998, Goldberg had to face six wrestlers before he got his shot at the Giant.

Battle Royale In this type of match, up to 24 wrestlers fight in the ring at the same time. The last man standing is the winner!

And that's what he did! Goldberg eliminated Scott Hall, Konnan, Curt Hennig, Scott Norton, Sting *and* Lex Luger before he confronted the Giant.

Goldberg took everything the Giant threw at him. He flattened the Giant with a Spear, then pinned him with a Jackhammer for the victory.

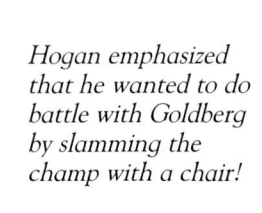

Hogan emphasized that he wanted to do battle with Goldberg by slamming the champ with a chair!

During this time, Hogan made it clear that he wanted to fight with Goldberg again. At a Monday Nitro, Hogan hit the champion with a chair. Kevin Nash, an nWo founder, pulled the chair away from Hogan. When Goldberg spotted Nash with the chair, he speared him, mistakenly thinking that Nash had hit him.

Goldberg had made a new enemy.

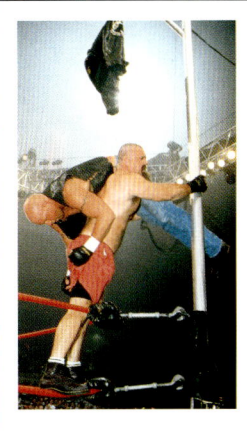

Skin's Match
WCW has seen wrestlers clash over unusual prizes — such as the "skin's match" where Tank Abbott battled Big Al over Al's beloved leather jacket!

Goldberg simply would not be intimidated by Hogan...or anyone else!

25

Causing havoc
Goldberg first caught the eye of WCW fans at Hallowe'en Havoc 1997, when he leapt into the ring and floored Steve McMichael.

Weeks later, the incident seemed forgotten. Goldberg and Nash paired up in a tag team match against Hogan and the Giant.

But during the battle, Nash jumped into the ring to help Goldberg, and ended up smashing him with his boot.

Was it an accident – or had Nash planned it? The tensions between Nash and Goldberg grew stronger.

At Hallowe'en Havoc that year, Goldberg fought his great friend, Diamond Dallas Page (*below*).

It was an epic battle. At first DDP trapped Goldberg in his famous Diamond Cutter; but with typical strength and skill, the champion broke free. Goldberg finally won, using the Jackhammer.

There was no bad feeling after the match. The close friends embraced in the spirit of sportsmanship that has always been the basis of Goldberg's career.

But as autumn changed to winter in 1998, a wrestler who cared little about sportsmanship prepared to end wrestling's greatest winning streak.

That wrestler was Kevin Nash.

Tag team
Two teams, of two wrestlers each, take part in a tag team match. The wrestlers take turns to battle or to rest.

Goldberg and DDP may be friends – but that doesn't stop DDP from trying any tactic to win their fights!

27

Anything goes
In a no-disqualification match, no holds are barred. No one can be disqualified for breaking the rules. The match ends when one of the wrestlers is unable to continue.

Losing
Goldberg thinks that the fight where he lost the championship was the strangest match he ever took part in. "What made it even stranger was that it happened on my birthday!" he says.

The streak ends

On 27 December 1998, Goldberg clashed with Kevin Nash in a "no-disqualification" match. The World Heavyweight Championship was on the line. So was Goldberg's streak of 175 victories in a row.

Goldberg fought bravely, even though at one stage he was battling Nash, Disco Inferno and Bam Bam Bigelow all at once.

Then Scott Hall entered the ring and hit Goldberg – with a stun gun. Goldberg collapsed to the mat. On a normal night, the challenger would have been disqualified for using a weapon. But not this night.

Goldberg had lost. Nash was the world champion.

Starrcade
Goldberg's incredible streak of victories finally came to an end during Starrcade 1998. The Starrcade event, which takes place in December, has been held since 1983. Goldberg has had other memorable Starrcades, including 1999 when he fought an epic battle with Bret Hart.

Kevin Nash jumps back just in time, as Goldberg lashes out.

The Rematch

In January 1999, Goldberg faced Nash in another "no disqualification" match. It was his attempt to regain the world title. But again, events were overtaken by an nWo plot.

Before the match began, the police arrested Goldberg. The nWo had laid false harrassment charges against him! When Goldberg finally returned to the arena, he was furious.

He found Hogan, Hall and other nWo members in the ring, celebrating his arrest. The former champ burst into the ring and pounded one foe after another.

But then Scott Hall brought out his stun gun. He knocked Goldberg out and painted "nWo" on his body.

Since then, Goldberg has fought to regain the world title many times.

Charges
Goldberg was arrested and charged with harrassing a woman. A live TV Nitro audience saw the police lead Goldberg away in handcuffs. Throughout the programme, the audience saw Goldberg being held at the police station, until he finally proved the charges were false, and returned to the ring.

He has not succeeded, although he did regain the WCW US title, in October 1999.

But being a winner is not just about titles. For his many fans, his decency, power, and spirit mean that Goldberg will always be a champion of champions.

Positive image
Asked if there was anything he would change about WCW, Goldberg speaks his mind: "If I could change one thing, it would be to kick out all the bad guys, so that we'd have nothing but fun, and present a positive image to kids."

Sid Vicious

Goldberg broke free of Sid Vicious' choke hold to regain the WCW US Championship title.

Lex Luger
Luger has won the WCW World Championship twice, as well as other titles.

Greatest foes

Goldberg has been wrestling for only a few years, but he has faced all the stars of the sport. Meet the rivals that he has wrestled on his way to the top.

Kevin Nash
Standing 2.1 m tall, and with a finishing move known as the Jack Knife Power Bomb, Kevin Nash is a wrestler to take very seriously! He has always been an outsider, and was a major member of the nWo, the rebel group that challenged WCW. A high point in his career was ending Goldberg's winning streak.

Kevin Nash has won the WCW World Heavyweight Championship title three times.

32

Scott Hall

Scott Hall is wrestling's hottest bad boy. He co-founded the nWo (New World Order), the rebel group that tried to overturn WCW. He considers himself an outlaw. And as he is over 1.92 m tall, no-one is going to argue with him!

Hall has been a professional wrestler since 1984, but his biggest impact has been within WCW. He fought and lost to Goldberg a number of times during Goldberg's winning streak. He then helped bring the streak to an end, when he brought a stun gun into the wrestling ring.

Billy Kidman
Kidman is one of the best athletes in wrestling. He combines a high-flying aerial style with classic mat moves.

Scott Steiner
The wrestler known as Big Poppa Pump was a wrestling champion in college. Steiner caused nothing but trouble for Goldberg and WCW when he joined up with the nWo.

Legendary
When people think of wrestling, they think of Hulk Hogan. No one believed that Goldberg could defeat him.

Hulk Hogan

He's the most famous wrestler of all time. He's also a film star, a former US presidential candidate, and the voice behind a famous cartoon character! Is there anything Hulk Hogan can't do? Since joining WCW in June 1994, he has earned eight World Championships titles. When he changed his name to "Hollywood Hogan", he adopted a mean identity and co-founded the nWo. He's now back to being the Hulkster, one of wrestling's all-time greats.

Diamond Dallas Page

This powerful wrestler finishes off his opponents with the Diamond Cutter, one of the most devastating finishing moves in wrestling. Yet, despite his fearsome power, Page is a likable "people's champion". He has had some unusual tag team partners, including the famous US basketball player Karl Malone.

Page, who is known as DDP, is a former wrestling manager and didn't start wrestling until he was in his 30s! He and Goldberg are two of WCW's "good guys". They are close friends, although their matches against each other have provided some of wrestling's greatest thrills.

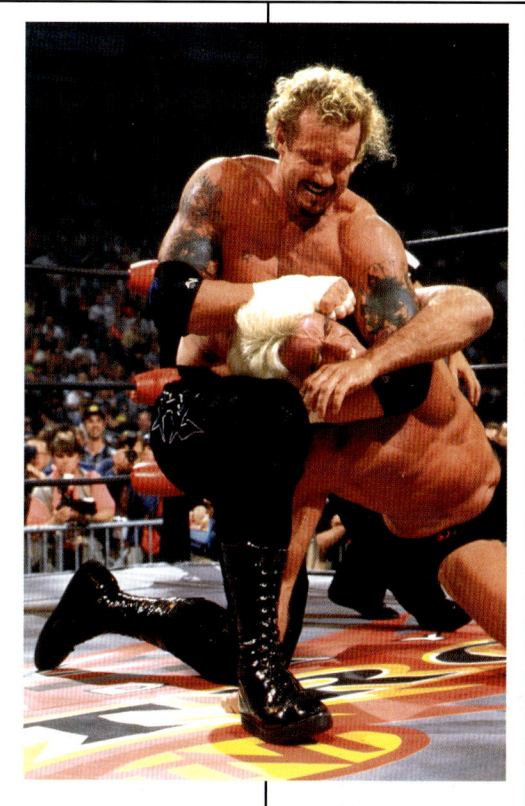

Buff Bagwell
Buff (*below*) has won three WCW World Tag Team titles, with three different partners.

35

Bam Bam Bigelow
Bam Bam is really scary! His huge head is covered with tattoos, adding to his overall air of menace.

Bret Hart

Bret "Hitman" Hart is the most famous Canadian wrestler in history. His father was a wrestler too, and obviously trained his son well, for Bret has held the World Heavyweight Title seven times.

His technical skill and toughness make the Hitman a powerful force. He has wrestled with Goldberg as a tag team partner, but he has also defeated the former champ during Goldberg's attempts to regain his world title.

When he's not winning matches, Hart is a columnist and cartoonist for the *Calgary Sun* newspaper.

Hart's finishing move, the Sharpshooter.

Sid Vicious

This ruthless bundle of raw power has torn through the world of wrestling. Demolishing his opponents with the Power Bomb, his finishing move, Sid became US and world champion. He put together a winning streak of over 150 matches, second only to Goldberg's. In fact, Goldberg ended Sid's winning streak.

When he's not wrestling, Sid loves to play softball. He even has a batting cage and pitching machine in his back yard.

Meng
Meng is expertly trained in nine forms of martial arts. His expertise and serious attitude make him a force to be reckoned with in WCW.

nWo havoc
Whenever one member of the nWo was in the ring, others were sure to follow. Kevin Nash (*below left*) sometimes stood by to watch while teammates such as Scott Hall (*right*) did their dirty work.

Toughest fights
Goldberg has fought some epic battles on his way to the top. His struggles against the nWo were some of the most exciting matches in WCW history. His clashes against Nash and Hogan have had WCW fans on the edge of their seats.

Recently, Goldberg was asked to pick his toughest opponent of all time. He chose Paul Wight – the Giant.

When the Giant fought in WCW, he was 2.1 m tall and weighed almost 230 kilos. He and Goldberg met many times.

Since the Jackhammer involves Goldberg lifting an opponent over his head, the champ wondered if he could even pick the Giant up. He did, again and again, beating the Giant each time in titanic battles.

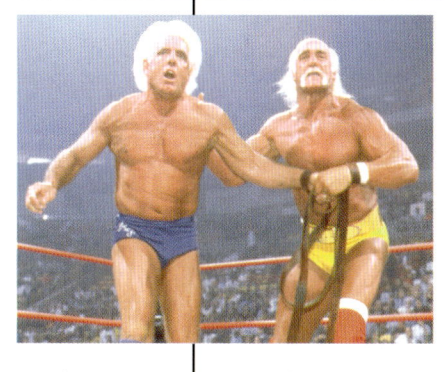

Lumberjack match
In this match, wrestlers stand outside the edge of the ring and throw back wrestlers trying to escape it!

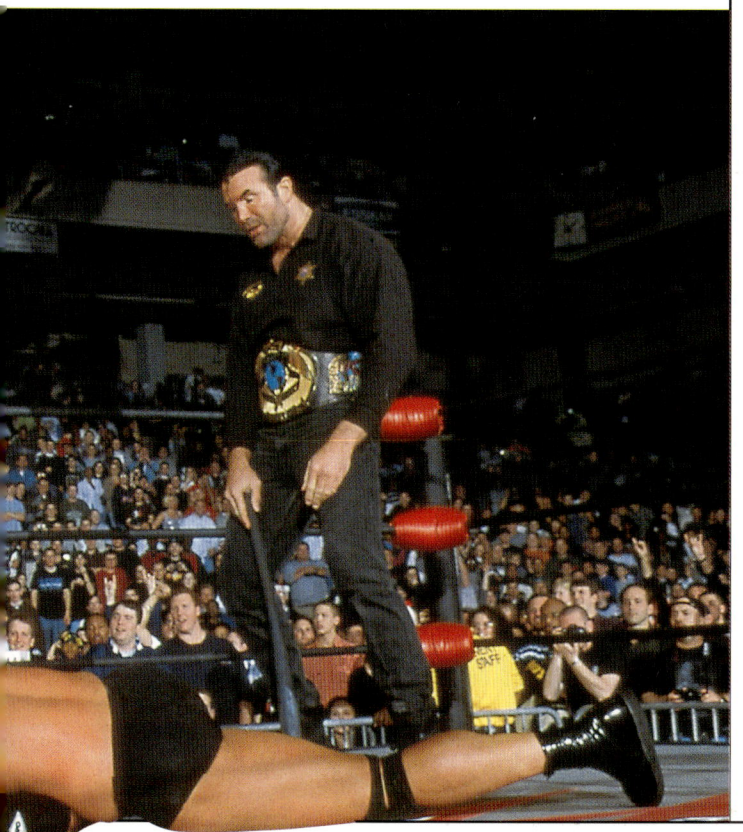

Own name
Many wrestlers take on bizarre nicknames, but Goldberg isn't one of them. "I decided to use my real name when I wrestled, so I could always be myself," he says.

Fitness routine

A muscular body like Goldberg's doesn't develop by accident. His sculpted physique is the result of hard work, commitment and hundreds of hours in the gym. To develop and maintain his body, Goldberg follows a regular routine.

"I exercise four or five days a week, for about an hour a day," Goldberg explains. "Two or three days a week, I do cardio kick-boxing. Cardio work is very important. It strengthens the heart and increases lung capacity, and keeps me from getting out of breath during a match."

But that's just the beginning.

"Four or five days a week I do a regular routine of weight training to keep my muscles strong," Goldberg continues. "Every other day, I concentrate on working my neck muscles to strengthen the Spear.

Food for life
A good diet is an important part of Goldberg's fitness routine. "I stay away from fatty foods and keep to a high protein, low-carbohydrate diet," he says.

The right stuff
Aspiring WCW heavyweight wrestlers must be aged between 18 to 28 and stand at least 1.75 m tall. Most weigh more than 82 kilos.

The rest of my fitness routine takes place in the ring. You might call it 'on-the-job' training."

Goldberg at work in the gym.

Self-belief
Goldberg is a role model to many young people, and he takes this responsibility seriously. "Don't let anybody ever tell you that you don't have the ability to do something," he says. "Don't sell yourself short. Always remember who you are and where you come from."

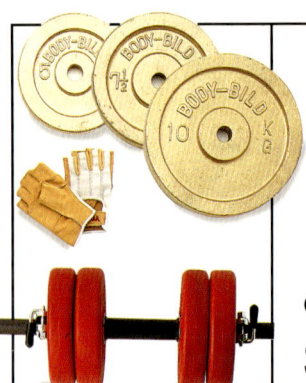

Weightlifting
Bodybuilders use free weights like these to define and shape their bodies.

Goldberg's hard work in the gym was never more important than when he injured a ligament in his knee during Slamboree, in May 1999. After surgery, he began the hard work to get his left leg back into shape.

A lot of the work focused on balance and stability. Strengthening the muscles around the ligament was vital to Goldberg's recovery, too.

Next came full-force kicks to heavy bags, the kind that boxers practise with. This helped build up power in Goldberg's leg.

As his knee improved, Goldberg wasn't happy with just returning to the fitness level he had before the injury. He wanted to go even further. He worked on a few new moves, including one called the Chainsaw.

All the hard work paid off. On Monday Nitro in July 1999, Goldberg returned to the ring. When the fireworks and smoke of his trademark entrance cleared, there stood Goldberg, the very picture of physical conditioning.

Dedication
Goldberg's former personal trainer, Timothy Catalfo, says, "Every single day, Bill Goldberg trains with the intensity of an 18-year-old trying to earn a scholarship for college. I've never seen someone fight so hard to improve himself."

Monster spirit
Catalfo himself is a former wrestler. Japanese fans gave him the nickname "Obake", meaning "spirit" and "monster", when he defeated 17 opponents in less than 35 minutes!

Merchandise
Toys and video games based on WCW heroes have always been popular. Now WCW is branching out and fans can buy everything from rock CDs to men's fragrances!

Goldberg in action in Universal Soldier, The Return.

On screen

Out of the arena, Goldberg has appeared on US television a number of times, with guest slots on popular shows such as *The Tonight Show with Jay Leno.*

He made his TV acting debut in *The Love Boat,* alongside Kevin Nash. They played tag team partners. The storyline centred around Goldberg getting married.

After Goldberg got a taste for acting, he wanted more. His first movie project was *Universal Soldier, The Return*. On that film, he worked with Jean Claude Van Damme, and played a character named Romeo.

His next project was a television film, *The Jesse Ventura Story*.

Most recently, he starred in the WCW and Warner Brothers' wrestling-based comedy, *Ready To Rumble*. Goldberg played a familiar role – one of the world's greatest wrestlers!

"I was always very curious about what it would be like to be in a movie," Goldberg says. "It was a great experience. I hope there are many more in the future."

Goldberg says he would love to become a movie actor when he retires from wrestling.

Ready to rumble
This comedy features many WCW stars. Most play themselves, but Kanyon (*above*) acted as stunt double for one of the lead actors, Oliver Platt. Super-fit Kanyon had to wear body padding to look more like the plump actor.

Helping out
Goldberg feels that his success and fame has given him something far more precious than money — the ability to help young people. "That's what I cherish more than anything else that I get from wrestling," he says. "It's an honour to be able to do what I do. It really is."

Big man, big heart

Goldberg loves children. "The best part of being Goldberg," he once said, "is being able to make a difference in a kid's life."

He has certainly done that. When he's not in the ring, you can usually find Goldberg helping out children's charities, like the Make-A-Wish Foundation. This organization grants the wishes of children who are very ill. Often, that wish is to meet a real-life superhero like Goldberg. He never lets them down.

He also helps raise money for the Starlight Foundation, which works for terminally ill children. Goldberg recently took part in an event that helped raise millions of pounds to build a new building for this charity.

In addition, Goldberg is a spokesman for the Humane Society, and speaks out for animal rights.

He tries to increase awareness on this issue and has even spoken about it to the US Congress.

There's no doubt about it. Goldberg is a true champion – both in and out of the ring!

Animal rights
Goldberg uses his popularity to get across the message of the Humane Society. The organization was founded in 1954 and exists to help protect all animals.

Glossary

Acrobatic
Daring and graceful, showing great skill and agility.

Advantage
A better position than someone else.

Aerial
In the air.

Attitude
The way a person views a situation.

Cardio
Related to strengthening the heart.

Columnist
A person who writes a regular feature for newspapers or magazines.

Confrontation
Facing someone with hostile intent.

Cunning
Clever or sly, someone who plans and plots.

Debut
The first time someone does something or something happens.

Dispose
Get rid of.

Disqualified
Declared the loser for breaking the laws or rules of a game.

Embrace
Hug.

Encourage
To push someone, in a positive way, to do something.

Feud
Quarrel or dispute.

Finishing move
The standard moves that a wrestler uses to win a match.

Formidable
Hard to overcome, inspiring fear or dread.

Glider
A small plane, with no engine, that rides the wind currents.

Martial arts
Self-defence techniques.

Opponent
A rival; someone who belongs to the opposite team.

Phenomenon
Remarkable person, event or thing.

Pin
In wrestling, to hold an opponent's shoulders to the mat for a count of three. This results in winning the match.

Psychology
The study of the mind and how it works.

Renegade
Someone who rejects rules and behaves poorly.

Ruthless
Not caring about anyone else. Mean and cruel.

Scout
A person representing a team, who watches an athlete and judges their ability to see if that athlete is right for his or her team.

Stable
Firmly in place.

Stun gun
A weapon used by police officers. It gives an electric shock that knocks out its victim.

Tag team
Usually, a team of two wrestlers. During a tag-team match, wrestlers from each team take it in turns to wrestle or to rest.